Careers in Biotechnology

Bonnie Szumski

San Diego, CA

About the Author

Bonnie Szumski has been an editor and author of nonfiction books for twenty-five years.

© 2015 ReferencePoint Press, Inc.
Printed in the United States

For more information, contact:
ReferencePoint Press, Inc.
PO Box 27779
San Diego, CA 92198
www. ReferencePointPress.com

Picture Credits:
Maury Aaseng: 6; © Jim Craigmyle/Corbis: 68; © Brownie Harris/Corbis: 11; © Michael Macor/San Francisco Chronicle/Corbis: 43

LIBRARY OF CONGRESS CATALOGING-IN-PUBLICATION DATA

Szumski, Bonnie, 1958– author.
  Careers in biotechnology / by Bonnie Szumski.
     pages cm — (Exploring careers)
  Includes bibliographical references and index.
  ISBN-13: 978-1-60152-702-8 (hardback)
  ISBN-10: 1-60152-702-0 (hardback)
  1. Biotechnology—Vocational guidance—Juvenile literature. I. Title.
  TP248.218.S98 2015
  660.6023—dc23
                                                                                              2014015009

Contents

Introduction

Solving Important Biological Problems

The field of biotechnology is both old and new. *Biotechnology* simply means to create technologies that are based on biology. These technologies and the products that result from them are developed through the use of cellular and biomolecular processes. Surprisingly, biotechnology has been around for more than six thousand years. Early humans used biotechnology to make cheese, for example, when they used living organisms to transform milk. Agriculture is just one of many fields that benefit from biotechnology. Biotechnology is also used in medicine, where it is applied toward the development of new drugs and medical treatments; in energy, where it is used to create cleaner, more efficient fuels; and in manufacturing, where it is employed in efforts to reduce pollution. According to the Biotechnology Industry Organization, "More than 250 biotechnology health care products and vaccines are now available to patients, many for previously untreatable diseases. More than 13.3 million farmers around the world use agricultural biotechnology to increase yields, prevent damage from insects and pests and reduce farming's impact on the environment. And more than 50 biorefineries are being built across North America to test and refine technologies to produce biofuels and chemicals from renewable biomass, which can help reduce greenhouse gas emissions."

The biotechnology industry is growing, and new companies are continually popping up to develop new products. This growth is likely to continue, as many of the problems that society will face in the next fifty years can be addressed through biotechnology. Just one example is that the baby boom generation is aging, and, as it does, significant medical problems are growing, including Alzheimer's, cancer, and obesity-related disease. New research into how and why these diseases occur—at the microscopic cellular level—is yielding results, and many biotech companies hope to offer more effective treatments based on these results. This is just one of many reasons that experts think the biotechnology market will be worth $1.2 trillion over the next four years—and that is likely to translate into jobs.

Many High-Paying Jobs

Most of the jobs produced by this industry are high paying, mainly because many of them require advanced degrees. The Bureau of Labor Statistics lists the field of biotechnology as growing at 31 percent through 2022, much faster than other fields, with a median salary of $79,000.

It is also a broadly defined industry, including professions such as biologist, pharmacist, chemist, and even brewer, food scientist, and cheese maker. Many biotechnology jobs, because of their technical nature, are bound to laboratories. Biotechnology jobs today are both tied to the laboratory and to the computer. Some careers, such as those in the bioinformatics industry, combine science with sophisticated computer software to crunch the mounds of data that are produced by researchers. Bioinformatics expert Ryan Brinkman, from Xenon Genetics in Vancouver, Canada, explains on bioteach.ubc.ca how bioinformatics allows researchers to be even more productive when sorting and evaluating their results: "Biologists have become really good at generating data. Biology has grown beyond the sticking pins into butterfly and placing them into a glass case stage. Now we sequence that butterfly's genome and put that data on the web for everyone to download. But once we have our huge pile of information (like DNA sequence), we need people who can put that butterfly sequence into a database, do the analysis and also put the raw data on the web so other biologists can also have access to it."

A Wide Variety of Career Options

A few of the careers in the biotechnology world do not take place mostly in the laboratory; some of these even require researchers to be detectives and adventure travelers. The role of epidemiologist, for

Biotechnology Occupations at a Glance: Educational Requirements and Wages

Key Occupation	Entry-Level Education	2012 First Quarter Wages	
		Median Hourly	Median Annual
Biochemical Engineers	3	$48.52	$100,936
Biochemists and Biophysicists	1	$39.19	$81,515
Biological Technicians	3	$21.45	$44,607
Biologists*	3	—	—
Biomedical Engineers	3	$47.05	$97,876
Chemical Engineers	3	$46.63	$96,992
Chemical Technicians	4	$21.16	$44,018
Chemists	3	$36.85	$76,659
Compliance Officers	3	$34.66	$72,086
Electrical Engineers	3	$49.13	$102,201
Environmental Scientists and Specialists, Including Health	3	$36.04	$74,978
Epidemiologists	2	$38.15	$79,354
Management Analysts	3	$40.60	$84,448
Market Research Analysts and Marketing Specialists	3	$32.74	$68,104
Medical and Clinical Laboratory Technicians	4	$19.61	$40,799
Medical and Clinical Laboratory Technologists	3	$38.97	$81,068
Medical Scientists, Except Epidemiologists	1	$40.12	$83,430
Microbiologists	3	$37.18	$77,332
Natural Sciences Managers	3	$68.79	$143,098
Statisticians	2	$43.13	$89,712
Technical Writers	3	$38.99	$81,101

Entry Level Education

1 Doctoral or professional degree **2** Master's degree **3** Bachelor's degree **4** Associate's degree

* Biologists include biochemists and biophysicists; microbiologists; zoologists and wildlife biologists; and biological scientists. Wage data is not published for this broader group.

Source: Employment Development Department, "Biotechnology in California," April 2013, p. 12.

example, is an unusual mix. Ali S. Khan, a field epidemiologist, says in an interview on the website microbeworld.org,

> My job is probably no different from any other detective in the world, except I try to figure out how people in a community are getting sick. What we do is we've got to find all the clues first. Then we've got to put all those little clues together like a puzzle to try to figure out what's going on in the community—who was the first person sick, who was the second, who was the third, what were their associations, what were the things that they did that got them infected. And the nice thing about what we do as disease detectives is that we don't just solve a mystery. Once we solve it, that tells us how we can actually make a difference—how we can make this disease go away.

Interestingly, many who have pursued a career in biotechnology relate that they did not know exactly what they wanted to become, they just followed their interests. Seth Darst is a professor of Molecular Biophysics at the Rockefeller University in New York City and was also interviewed on microbeworld.com. He says, "If I had the time and I told you the story of my career, the striking thing about it is that it's sort of been one random thing after another. I think students should just go with the flow and do what you find interesting at the moment and it will work out."

For someone interested in science and technology, with a desire to understand how life works at its most basic level along with a willingness to spend significant time in academia, a biotechnology career might be the right choice. One thing is for sure, working in the field of biotechnology means solving some of the most important issues facing people in the twenty-first century.

Biochemist

Biochemists work in a variety of jobs in medicine (including veterinary medicine), nutrition, and agriculture. In all of these areas the work of a biochemist is primarily research in an academic or lab setting. Biochemists study chemical reactions in metabolism, growth, reproduction, and heredity. In the lab their duties include culturing, filtering, drying, weighing, and measuring substances using instruments of their trade. Their work combines the disciplines of chemistry and biology. As editor for *BMC Biochemistry* magazine Sabato D'Auria says on biomedcentral.com, "What is exciting is that more than other research areas, in chemical biology the fields of chemistry and biology are strongly intertwined and so researchers must have an interdisciplinary approach. Chemical biology involves the application of chemical techniques, tools, or compounds to the study and manipulation of biological systems."

In the medical field biochemists are heavily involved in the study of disease and its origin, spread, prevention, and treatment. Biochemists may study

At a Glance:
Biochemist

Minimum Educational Requirements
Bachelor's degree in biochemistry; advanced degrees common

Personal Qualities
Detail oriented; methodical; inquiring mind; good at science and math; logical thinker

Certification and Licensing
None

Working Conditions
Indoors in a research laboratory

Salary Range
From about $81,480 to $147,350

Number of Jobs
As of 2012 about 29,200

Future Job Outlook
Expected 19 percent growth through 2022

the chemical changes in organs and cells that signal the onset of a particular disease. They may study the chemical makeup of people with a particular disease. For example, biochemists have studied autism in an attempt to learn why certain children are more prone to developing the syndrome. Biochemists involved in this research sought to understand why children with autism seemed to have higher levels of heavy metals in their bodies, even though they had no more exposure to heavy metals than other children. (Heavy metals occur naturally in the environment. Exposure to very small quantities of heavy metals is common. Some, such as iron, copper, and zinc, are found in fruits and vegetables and are essential to good health.) Through their work biochemists have found that autistic children seem to have lower-than-normal quantities of a chemical that helps the body eliminate heavy metals. Biochemists are also involved in the study of AIDS. They were instrumental in discovering how the virus evaded the immune system, and they continue to be involved in the development of a vaccine.

The work of biochemists can also be seen in efforts to develop new drugs and medical devices. They work to artificially produce drugs that mimic natural chemicals such as hormones or enzymes that might be lacking in the body. They are also involved in the quality control of a drug, what the dosage should be, and how the drug should be taken. And they study and isolate chemical compounds in an attempt to come up with new treatments. In a recent discovery, biochemists found that a chemical in leftover beer hops is the same chemical used to treat gum disease. This discovery could lead to a periodontal treatment that could be cheaply obtained from the thousands of tons of waste created in the making of beer. In another example, professor and biochemist Steve O'Rahilly is well known for his research into genetic disorders and the resulting treatments discovered through his research. He is one of the scientists who has proved a link between biochemistry and obesity. In an interview for the National Institutes of Health website he talks about how excited he feels when his research leads to a new treatment: "I'm feeling very bullish at the moment, because there's a child I went to see . . . some 12 years ago and we've been struggling all these years to understand what's going on with [his] particular condition. . . . It's early days yet, but as of last week we've got the answer, and it's beautiful. It's a generalisable story and it's one we think we may be able to get a therapy for. So that's the excitement—you can find things that are elegant, but also that you can do something about."

In the field of nutrition biochemists work in many industries to isolate how food affects body function. For example, biochemist Roselle Rojas, in an interview on YouTube, describes her work at the Gatorade company. In order to develop effective sports nutrition drinks that replenish needed electrolytes and other trace minerals, Rojas studies the chemical composition of the sweat of athletes after activity. She also monitors other biochemical changes in an athlete's body by collecting samples of other bodily fluids. Biochemists also study vitamin and mineral deficiencies and attempt to understand how these affect people and how they can be chemically replenished. Biochemists have also helped produce a highly nutritious, high-calorie food product that can feed people suffering from starvation, for example.

In agriculture biochemists are involved in the development of plants, understanding the diseases that affect them, and seeking ways to make plants grow faster and stronger. They work on developing genetically engineered crops, for example, that can resist insects and diseases. Biochemists were involved in the development of plant fungicides to inhibit fungi from attacking plants. They were also involved in the development of chemical fertilizers.

How Do You Become a Biochemist?

Education

People who hold entry-level jobs in biochemistry typically have a bachelor of science degree in biochemistry, molecular biology, or life science. Biotechnology companies recommend that students choose a program certified by the American Chemical Society. These degrees include the study of organic and physical chemistry, calculus, and biochemistry. In order to obtain higher level jobs, a master's degree in biochemistry or science is helpful, as many employers prefer that a candidate have a research-based master's degree. A biochemist with a

One of the areas biochemists work in is pharmaceutical research (pictured). Whichever field they work in, their research involves a combination of chemistry and biology.

master's degree will still typically work under a senior scientist. In order to become a senior scientist a doctorate is required. The advantage to this level of education is the ability to design research projects and to also supervise other scientists. Many biochemists go on to earn a doctorate in biochemistry, chemistry, or a related field. For this level of career, employers prefer candidates who have several years of experience in postdoctoral research.

Sihong Chen argues on the website ucd.ie that pursuing a degree in biochemistry opens an exciting career path for a student: "Everything in our world is linked to science and technology, and by choosing science, you give yourself the opportunity not only to understand how things in the world work, but also to be able to make your own contribution to society. If you are curious about the world around you, and are looking for an exciting career path with opportunities that you may never have considered, then I would definitely suggest choosing science and biochemistry in particular!"

Certification and Licensing

To work in certain settings, such as hospitals, biochemists may be required to obtain a certificate from the American Board of Clinical Chemistry.

Volunteer Work and Internships

Internships in research are typically given to current students or recent graduates in degree programs. Private labs, federal and state governments, the National Institutes of Health, and branches of the military all offer paid internships to undergraduates in biochemistry. For PhD candidates such research is a requirement for getting a job, as most employers prefer that candidates have practical research experience. Biochemistry professors at many universities offer mostly paid postdoctoral research positions in their laboratories to new graduates from PhD programs.

Skills and Personality

Biochemistry is similar to other degrees in science in that a person must be scientifically minded and logical in his or her thinking. Biochemists are familiar with the methods of experimentation as well as of drawing conclusions from experiments and extrapolating from those conclusions possible solutions to problems. They must also have excellent oral and written communication skills, as their research and ideas must be communicated to others on their team as well as published in scientific papers and delivered at professional conferences. In general, a passion for the sciences and working in a lab are musts. On the ucd.ie website Chen talks about the qualities that led her to pursue a PhD in biochemistry: "I was always fascinated by the world around me and saw science as mysterious and powerful. In high school, I realized that I had a real passion for science and started to consider entering science as a career. There are still many questions today that we don't have the answers for e.g., scientists have solved the DNA sequence of the human gene, but 50% of genes' functions are still unknown. Diseases such as cancer and HIV are much better understood, still we don't know how to cure them. These questions are still waiting for future scientists to answer."

On brightknowledge.org, biochemist Janusz Knepil talks about the skills needed in his area of expertise, which is the study of diseases and possible treatments. He argues that the primary skill is: "Determination and an ability to be close to other people's tragedy without allowing [it] to overcome you. Although you can be and are sympathetic, too much pity is neither useful nor appreciated but comes over as patronizing. It is necessary, therefore to develop a sense of realism without becoming hardened."

On the Job

Employers

According to the Bureau of Labor Statistics, biochemists were employed by the following industries in 2012:

- Research and development in the physical, engineering, and life sciences: 47 percent.
- Colleges, universities, and professional schools (state, local, and private): 17 percent.
- Pharmaceutical and medicine manufacturing: 14 percent.
- Drugs and druggists' sundries merchant wholesalers: 2 percent.
- Testing laboratories: 2 percent.

Texas A&M University Career Fair's website lists dozens of companies seeking biochemists. Among them are the Army Medical Department, MD Anderson Cancer Center, Proctor and Gamble, and the Texas Department of Public Safety Crime Lab.

Working Conditions

Biochemists typically work in laboratories and offices to conduct experiments and analyze the results. Most biochemists work on research teams, often with a variety of scientists from different fields including physics, computer science, and engineering. They can work with dangerous substances. They usually have regular hours with little overtime.

Earnings

According to the Bureau of Labor Statistics, in 2012 the median annual wages for biochemists in the top five areas of employment were:

- Drugs and druggists' sundries merchant wholesalers: $103,390.
- Research and development in the physical, engineering, and life sciences: $86,530.
- Pharmaceutical and medicine manufacturing: $82,490.
- Testing laboratories: $74,230.
- Colleges, universities, and professional schools (state, local, and private): $52,990.

Opportunities for Advancement

Advancement opportunities for biochemists typically follow from more education. Those with doctorates can advance the highest, becoming lead scientists on research projects that they design and supervise. Prestige and more job opportunities can also follow from working on high-profile projects with a lot of public and commercial interest, such as new medical treatments, new drugs, and breakthroughs in research.

What Is the Future Outlook for Biochemists?

According to the Bureau of Labor Statistics, employment of biochemists is projected to grow by 19 percent through 2022, which amounts to about fifty-four hundred new jobs. The field of biomedical research is expected to grow in particular as the baby boom generation ages and new treatments for diseases become more important. Genetic research, as well, will continue to be an important employment area for biochemists as technologies allow for more in-depth research at the cell level. The development of new fuels and the need for technology to solve environmental problems will also be areas of growth.

Find Out More

American Association for Clinical Chemistry (AACC)
1850 K St. NW, Suite 625
Washington, DC 20006
phone: (800) 892-1400
website: aacc.org

AACC is an international scientific/medical society of professionals involved with clinical chemistry and related disciplines. AACC publishes the journal *Clinical Chemistry*, the most cited in the field. AACC offers many programs that address the scientific, clinical, technical, and management challenges facing laboratory professionals.

American Society for Biochemistry and Molecular Biology (ASBMB)
11200 Rockville Pike, Suite 302
Rockville, MD 20852-3110
phone: (240) 283-6600
website: ASBMB.org

The ASBMB is a nonprofit scientific and educational organization. Its purpose is to advance the science of biochemistry and molecular biology through publication of scientific and educational journals. ASBMB also organizes scientific meetings, advocates for funding of basic research and education, and supports science education at all levels.

American Society for Pharmacology and Experimental Therapeutics
9650 Rockville Pike
Bethesda, MD 20814-3995
website: aspet.org

The American Society for Pharmacology and Experimental Therapeutics (ASPET) is a scientific society whose members conduct basic and clinical pharmacological research in academia, industry, and the government. Members' research efforts help develop new medicines and therapeutic agents to fight existing and emerging diseases.

Federation of American Societies for Experimental Biology (FASEB)
9650 Rockville Pike
Bethesda, MD 20814
phone: (301) 634-7000
website: faseb.org

The Federation of American Societies for Experimental Biology provides a forum in which to hold educational meetings, develop publications, and disseminate biological research results. FASEB is recognized as the policy voice of biological and biomedical researchers.

Epidemiologist

Epidemiologists are detectives of disease. When an outbreak of a disease occurs, epidemiologists attempt to figure out its cause, how and why it is spreading, how to stop it, and, ultimately, how to contain and prevent it from happening again. They also use statistical analysis to figure out who is at risk and why. For example, if an outbreak of illness caused by *E. coli* occurs in a city, doctors will report the cases to the Centers for Disease Control and Prevention (CDC). CDC epidemiologists will collect the data and try to identify similarities among the people who came down with the disease. Did they all eat raw spinach, for example? Did they all eat at a particular restaurant where they had a similar meal? Once the common cause is identified, epidemiologists figure out what the food danger is. In the case of raw spinach, what brand of raw spinach was it? Did all of the spinach come from a particular vendor? Where was it grown? After tallying all of the results of their fact gathering, epidemiologists contact the offending producer, who is usually shut down until the food issue is remedied. As epidemiologist Atif Kukaswadia says

At a Glance:
Epidemiologist

Minimum Educational Requirements
Master's degree, usually in public health

Personal Qualities
Analytical and logical mind; good oral and written communication skills; good research skills

Certification and Licensing
Optional

Working Conditions
Indoors in a lab; some on-site work may be involved

Salary Range
From about $42,620 to $108,320

Number of Jobs
As of 2012 about 5,100

Future Job Outlook
Ten percent growth through 2022

on queensu.com, "In short—Epidemiologists study who is getting sick, what is making them sick, and how sick they are getting."

Epidemiologists work all over the world, studying populations of people who have a larger than normal incidence of a particular disease. They gather data, sometimes over long periods of time, and make suggestions to stem the disease. Epidemiologist Jill Koshiol talks about her average workday on nihlifeworks.org: "My typical day is spent sitting in front of the computer to learn about current and past research by finding and reviewing published studies, writing proposals for new research projects, analyzing data, writing papers describing my results, and communicating and coordinating my research via email. I also attend meetings to discuss my projects and learn about science. No matter how much I know, there's always more to learn."

Epidemiologists work closely with state and federal governments. Almost all nations have a national disease surveillance program to keep track of disease data. There is even an international agreement headed by the World Health Organization in Geneva, Switzerland, to report three diseases—cholera, plague, and yellow fever—so that a world watch on these dangerous diseases is monitored. In the United States the CDC, US Public Health Service, and the state health officers of all fifty states have agreed to report the occurrence of fifty-one diseases weekly and of another ten diseases annually to the CDC. Many states have regulations or laws that mandate reporting these diseases and often other diseases of specific interest to the state health department. Epidemiologists use this data to help them when a particular disease or a new disease becomes a problem.

Epidemiologists study the chain of infection. This includes the cause, or etiologic agent, the method of transmission, and the host. The etiologic agent is analyzed to determine its severity and at what rate people die of the infection. For example, the agent of the plague, *Yersinia pestis*, almost always causes severe disease that is lethal. Epidemiologists also study the method of transmission, which is the means by which an agent infects the host.

AIDS provides a good example of how epidemiologists study a disease. At first, epidemiologists did not know what was causing AIDS or even that it was a common syndrome. The first cases in 1981 had common symptoms, including fever, loss of appetite, weight loss, and fatigue. As the disease progressed, other secondary infections appeared. These included pneumonia, a type of skin lesion called Karposi's sarcoma, and other parasitic, bacterial, and viral infections. The presence of these infections suggested the disease was compromising the immune system of those who had the illness. Epidemiologists tracked the number of cases of this developing disease and how many patients developed which symptoms. According to the National Institutes of Health, among the first 2,640 cases reported to the CDC, there were 1,092 deaths, a fatality rate of 41 percent. Approximately 95 percent of the cases were male; 70 percent were twenty to forty-nine years of age at the time of diagnosis. Approximately 40 percent of the cases were reported from New York City, 12 percent from San Francisco, 8 percent from Los Angeles, and the remainder from thirty-two other states. Cases were reported from at least sixteen other countries. Among the 90 percent of patients who were categorized according to possible risk factors, those at highest risk were homosexuals or bisexuals (70 percent), intravenous drug abusers (17 percent), Haitians who had come into the United States (9.5 percent), and persons with hemophilia (1 percent).

By examining these trends, epidemiologists understood that AIDS was caused by sexual contact or contaminated blood. Epidemiologists eventually narrowed down the cause of AIDS to a virus, which they named human immunodeficiency virus, or HIV.

How Do You Become an Epidemiologist?

Education

Epidemiologists can have degrees in a wide range of specialties, though a master's degree in public health with an emphasis in epidemiology is most common. A PhD is required if an epidemiologist is in charge of a research project or teaches in a college or university. Budding epidemiologists study public health, the biological and physical sciences, math, and statistics. Math is a large part of an epidemiologist's work, and courses include statistical methods, causal analysis, and survey design. Some epidemiologists also obtain a medical degree. During their master's program epidemiologists are often required to complete a semester or year-long internship as well.

In the July 2010 issue of *Epidemiology*, long-time epidemiologist Lew Kuller talks about the path he took to this line of work:

> I started out in the early 1960s in internal medicine. I spent time in the emergency room and especially on ambulance call in New York City. While doing that, I recognized the high frequency of sudden deaths in the community, most of which we attributed to coronary heart disease. It intrigued me that we didn't know very much about these—it seemed more people were dying of heart attacks out of the hospital than in the hospital. I then went into the Navy. While I was in the Navy, I got interested in the idea of doing chronic disease research. After I was discharged, I applied to Johns Hopkins to work in the Program in Chronic Diseases at the Moore Clinic.

Certification and Licensing

Certification is voluntary, although some in the field say it demonstrates to potential employers greater commitment to the job. Certification is available through an exam offered by the Certification Board of Infectious Control and Epidemiology. Certification is good for five years.

Volunteer Work and Internships

Almost all epidemiologist candidates volunteer for or are required to perform a semester or year-long internship while still in graduate school. Many public health institutions offer internships, including the CDC and World Health Organization. Many colleges and universities offer internships around the world.

Skills and Personality

Epidemiologists must have a variety of personality and skill sets. On the one hand, they must be analytical and detail oriented. They have to like math and science and have an interest in data crunching, analyzing numbers, and working with mathematical rubrics to understand patterns of disease. They must also enjoy higher education and research, since a career as an epidemiologist requires at least a master's degree. On the other hand, epidemiology is one of the caring professions. Depending on where and what they are researching, they may need to interview hundreds of sick people to understand their disease and how they were exposed. They must have excellent oral and written communication skills because they often work with a variety of people from many different socioeconomic backgrounds. On the website whatispublichealth.org, state epidemiologist and director of the Office of Epidemiology of New Mexico C. Mack Sewell talks about why he chose this career: "I found in the field of epidemiology a way to combine my interests in science, human health, microbiology and infectious diseases into one powerful discipline. That was tremendously appealing to me. There is a certain thrill about working as an epidemiologist. In this field we are identifying risk factors that can lead to effective interventions before the etiology of a disease or condition is fully understood."

On the Job

Employers

According to the Bureau of Labor Statistics, 52 percent of epidemiologists work for state and local governments (such as public health departments). This figure does not include epidemiologists working in colleges and universities or hospitals, which also employ epidemiologists. Pharmaceutical companies are yet another employer in this field.

Working Conditions

Most epidemiologists work in a lab setting with data sets. Some work in the field gathering data. On nihlifeworks.org Koshiol speaks of what she likes best and least about the working conditions: "What I like best about my work is the feeling of contributing to the understanding of cancer through my research at the National Cancer Institute. . . . What I like least about my work is administrative details. There is a lot of paper work and processes to complete for any given project. A project has to be approved by many scientific review committees before we can begin, and the review process can take time."

Some epidemiologists, however, find themselves working in the field. Epidemiologist Dale Morse found out how rewarding a career in the field could be while volunteering at a Navajo Indian reservation after his first year of medical school at the University of Rochester in New York. He also volunteered at the local county health department to find out more about the public health aspect of epidemiology. While there, Morse witnessed two minor health issues that involved the type of investigative work that epidemiologists do. The first was a small number of cases that were eventually blamed on an allergic reaction among children to a dye in popular "tattoos" they bought. The second was a large outbreak of giardiasis, an illness that is caused by a parasite in contaminated water. The outbreak was reported to and investigated by the CDC. The investigating Epidemic Intelligence Service (EIS) officer invited Morse to assist with the investigation. The episode made him realize the importance of the career. On sciencebuddies.com Morse comments on the fieldwork aspect of the job: "Working through a disaster is like transitioning from working on a general medical floor to a busy hospital emergency room. You're doing some of the same things you might do in your routine as an epidemiologist, but everything is intensely time-driven."

Earnings

According to the Bureau of Labor Statistics, the median annual wage for epidemiologists was $65,270 in May 2012. Incomes varied according to where an epidemiologist worked. Research and development in the physical, engineering, and life sciences paid $92,070; general medical and surgical hospitals (state, local, and private) paid $ 73,810; colleges, universities, and professional schools (state, local, and private) paid $66,960; while state and local government agencies (excluding colleges and hospitals) paid $59,090.

Opportunities for Advancement

Epidemiologists can advance by earning an MD or PhD, which allows them to take on positions with greater responsibilities. An epidemiologist who is also an MD can administer drugs during clinical trials, for example. The highest paying positions are those in the research field, though these are highly coveted and competition is fierce.

What Is the Future Outlook for Epidemiologists?

Employment of epidemiologists is projected to grow by 10 percent through 2022, according to the Bureau of Labor Statistics. The bureau states that improved methods of data collection will make epidemiologists more valuable to state and local governments and increase job availability.

Find Out More

Centers for Disease Control and Prevention
1600 Clifton Rd.
Atlanta, GA 30333
phone: (800) 232-4636
website: www.cdc.gov

The mission of the CDC is to collaborate with other organizations in the health care field to create the expertise, information, and tools that people and communities need to protect their health—through health promotion; prevention of disease, injury, and disability; and preparedness for new health threats.

Council of State and Territorial Epidemiologists (CSTE)
2872 Woodcock Blvd., Suite 250
Atlanta, GA 30341
phone: (770) 458-3811
website: www.cste.org

CSTE works to advance public health policy and epidemiologic capacity. It also provides information, education, and developmental support of practicing epidemiologists in a wide range of areas as well as expertise for program and surveillance efforts.

National Institutes of Health (NIH)
31 Center Dr.
Bethesda, MD 20892
phone: (301) 496-4000
website: www.nih.gov

Part of the US Department of Health and Human Services, the NIH is the nation's premier medical research agency. NIH's mission is to seek fundamental knowledge about the nature and behavior of living systems and the application of that knowledge to enhance health, lengthen life, and reduce illness and disability.

World Health Organization (WHO)
Avenue Appia 20
1211 Geneva 27
Switzerland
phone: + 41 22 791 21 11
website: www.who.int

WHO is the directing and coordinating authority for health within the United Nations system. It is responsible for providing leadership on global health matters, shaping the health research agenda, setting norms and standards, articulating evidence-based policy options, providing technical support to countries, and monitoring and assessing health trends.

Biomedical Engineer

Biomedical engineering is a relatively new field, and much of the work these engineers do is cutting-edge. Biomedical engineers have been involved in the mapping of the human genome; the development of robotics; the engineering of body tissues, including artificial organs; and nanotechnology. They are responsible for finding ways to make adult stem cells function like fetal stem cells. They have developed advanced artificial limbs that respond to signals from the brain. They are responsible for the treatment of many diseases, including brain implants that help Parkinson's patients communicate and calm tremors. They have even been involved in agriculture and the design of genetically engineered crops. In the broadest sense, biomedical engineers solve problems related to biology and medicine. They may design instruments, devices, and software or conduct research or design ways to test new drugs or medical devices. They also design rehabilitative exercise equipment.

At a Glance:
Biomedical Engineer

Minimum Educational Requirements
Bachelor's degree

Personal Qualities
Must have an excellent grasp of and enjoy the sciences, math, and chemistry; enjoy learning and problem solving

Certification and Licensing
Voluntary

Working Conditions
Indoors

Salary Range
About $59,000 to $88,330

Number of Jobs
As of 2013 about 15,700 in the United States

Future Job Outlook
Much better than average; growth rate of 62 percent through 2020

To perform their job, biomedical engineers must understand human biology and technology.

These engineers often must combine areas of expertise in their daily work. For example, designing computer software to run complicated medical instruments requires programming knowledge as well as an understanding of the mechanics behind medical devices. Likewise, engineers who work on drug therapies must have knowledge of chemistry and biology. They usually work as part of a team that includes people with medical expertise in the field they are working in. The profession of biomedical engineer has many specialties:

- Bioinstrumentation engineers work on devices that diagnose and treat disease. In this arena, knowledge of computers is essential.
- Biomaterials engineers design, test, and research materials that will be used in the replacement of living tissue and implants. They must test these materials for safety, endurance, and strength. They must also make sure that these materials will not have an adverse reaction in the body.
- Biomechanics engineers use their knowledge of mechanics and apply that knowledge to the body to better understand how these areas intersect and how they can be used together to improve quality of life. Biomechanical engineers sometimes work on products and treatments related to one particular part of the body, such as the cardiovascular system.
- Cellular, tissue, and genetics engineers work at the cellular level to understand how diseases attack the cells and how to intervene to help those cells fight off disease.
- Clinical engineers are hired by hospitals to help purchase medical instruments and adapt those instruments to respond to the needs of physicians and the hospital. They must understand and maintain advanced medical machinery and have knowledge of computer instrumentation.
- Medical imaging engineers develop diagnostic equipment that produces images that doctors can interpret and understand in order to treat patients. They must understand the principles of sound, radiation, and magnetism.

- Orthopedic engineers design artificial joints and study the way joints move.
- Rehabilitation engineers design and develop artificial limbs and rehabilitative equipment.
- Systems physiology engineers develop and design computer models to analyze data related to the way living organisms function. They work at the microscopic level and may study skin and how it heals itself or responds to a particular drug.

Lori Laird is a biomedical engineer who designs noninvasive instruments and tools for use by vascular surgeons in the treatment of blocked arteries. She also works with manufacturing personnel on issues of design for manufacturing and quality control. When asked what her typical day is like on the website TryEngineering, Laird replies:

Yesterday was a good day. I did a lot of different things yesterday. I started out with a meeting. Actually, I started out checking out e-mail and voice mail and writing myself my "to do" list for today; these are the things I'm going to accomplish. I went to a meeting in the morning. After that, I went to a class where they teach about the safety of blood-borne pathogens. In medical devices, there are a lot of safety and medical issues. We handle devices as they come back from the field to check them out for defects and things like that. And I took a class on how to handle the devices and not get contaminated by the blood. After that, I checked out one of the tools. We're having a problem with one of our tools on the manufacturing line. So I sat down, I called the vendor and talked to them about different ways to make this tool. Did a little bit of designing.

How Do You Become a Biomedical Engineer?

Education

High school students interested in a biomedical engineering career need to take science, chemistry, physics, and biology courses. In addition, courses in higher mathematics such as algebra and calculus are good options. Those students interested in the design part of this discipline would benefit from drafting, mechanical drawing, or computer programming courses as well.

Students who pursue this major in college need to find a degree program that is accredited by the Accreditation Board for Engineering and Technology. Degree programs focus on engineering coupled with the biological sciences—such as physiology, pharmacology, and biology. These courses also require hours in a laboratory. Other courses that may be included are fluid and solid mechanics, computer programming, circuit design, and biomaterials.

Many students go on to pursue postgraduate education in a particular field of bioengineering. These students often learn more practical application of their education by working with a faculty member on a project or research experiment.

Certification and Licensing

As with other engineering careers, certification is required if the engineer is planning on working on projects that affect the health, safety, or life of the public. They must attain a Professional Engineering license. Such a license is required by all fifty states and Washington, DC.

Volunteer Work and Internships

High school students interested in this career should apply for internships at hospitals. In addition, participating in science fairs is a good way to learn about developing products or designing research. Undergraduate students in accredited programs are offered many opportunities for volunteer programs, many of which include internships at hospitals.

Skills and Personality

A love of continual education is a good quality for a biomedical engineer. Since the career is in constant flux as new technologies are developed, biomedical engineers must learn new techniques and systems. Biomedical engineers must be able to analyze the needs of patients and customers to design appropriate solutions. Although all engineers require good analytical, math, science, and communication skills as well as a love of problem solving, biomedical engineers must have other qualities as well. Because they work on diverse teams that may include patients, therapists, physicians, and businesspeople, biomedical engineers must have good listening skills to address the needs of these various stakeholders. In addition, biomedical engineers work with biological systems, so they need to be adept both at mechanical applications and the science of the human body.

Laird describes how she got into the biomedical field. She started out as a mechanical engineer.

> I grew up in Los Angeles, Southern California. Started going to school at Long Beach State. And at the time, I still didn't know I wanted to be a mechanical engineer. I tried zoology, because I liked animals. I tried architecture. And then I still wasn't satisfied. And so I took an aptitude test from the career center at Long Beach State, and they said, "By golly, you should be an engineer." And I always kind of thought in the back of my head that that's what I wanted to do. But I just needed somebody to tell me. And I decided to do mechanical engineering because I've always enjoyed taking things apart. Solving puzzles, solving problems. I enjoy picturing things spatially and in 3D and things like that. And that really drove me down the path of mechanical engineering.

Laird always wanted to be in the biomedical engineering field, but her school did not offer a program specifically for that field, so she had to find another way to do it: "I did an emphasis on biomedical. I took more design classes. I took extra biology classes, physiology. . . . I kind of had to create my own degree. And I did senior projects in that area. Did design projects involving biomedical or prosthetics and things like that."

On the Job

Employers

About 15,700 biomedical engineers work in the United States. According to the Bureau of Labor Statistics, most biological engineers—23 percent—work in the medical equipment and manufacturing sector. Scientific research and development makes up 19 percent of the biomedical engineering jobs in the United States, and pharmaceutical and medicine manufacturing make up 14 percent. Academia makes up another 11 percent, with biomedical engineers working at colleges, universities, and professional schools. State, local, and private government jobs make up 11 percent, and general medical and surgical hospitals hold 7 percent.

Biomedical engineers work in many different settings, and much depends on which specialty they are in. Some work in hospitals where therapy occurs, and others work in laboratories doing research. Those with design skills may work in manufacturing.

Working Conditions

Though biomedical engineers mostly work inside in one location, some are required to travel. Biomedical engineers who work with medical machinery, such as imaging machinery, or with products that affect patients, such as prosthetics, may be required to work on-site testing the new equipment or working with patients who receive the prosthetic devices. They often team up with other professionals when they work directly with patients. As with many other engineering professions, biomedical engineers spend a lot of time working on a single problem. Mark Pagel has been a professor of biomedical engineering at the University of Arizona since 2008. On the website Colleges & Degrees, he explains the importance of being both persistent and patient: "Perseverance is critical in all fields of science and engineering. Research is difficult and many small techniques need to be successful for an entire research experiment to be successful. There is simply no substitute to trying again and again until the experiment is successful. Thomas Edison's perseverance in creating the light bulb is perhaps the best example." He also remarks that writing is important to the profession: "Technical writing is also critical. Biomedical engineers who have the personality traits to communicate their research, and to refine their skills in writing and oral presentations, have a clear advantage."

Earnings

The median annual wage of biomedical engineers was $81,540 in 2010, according to the Bureau of Labor Statistics. The top 10 percent in the profession earned more than $126,990. Because of the many specialties involved, salaries vary among the sectors in which biomedical engineers might work. According to the Bureau of Labor Statistics, wages are as follows: scientific research and development services, $88,330; pharmaceutical and medicine manufacturing, $82,820; medical equipment and supplies manufacturing, $81,150; colleges, universities, and professional schools—state, local, and private, $68,070; general medical and surgical hospitals—state, local, and private, $59,010.

Opportunities for Advancement

Many biological engineers go on to earn postgraduate degrees in medicine or other specialties. Salaries are tied to these advanced degrees—the higher the level of education an engineer has attained, the higher his or her pay.

What Is the Future Outlook for Biomedical Engineers?

The outlook is very good for biomedical engineers. The Bureau of Labor Statistics expects this field to grow by 62 percent through 2020, much more quickly than other engineering professions. However, because the field is more specialized, the number of jobs in this field is small to begin with. So even though it is a growing field, there will still be a small total number of jobs.

Increase in demand is tied to the aging baby boomer generation, who will require more prosthetics and implants as they age. In addition, new medical advances are continually being researched and designed, further enhancing the need for such engineers.

Find Out More

American Institute for Medical and Biological Engineering (AIMBE)
1701 K St. NW, Suite 510
Washington, DC 20006
phone: (202) 496-9660
website: www.aimbe.org

The AIMBE is a nonprofit organization headquartered in Washington, DC. It represents fifty thousand individuals and the top 2 percent of medical and biological engineers. In addition, the AIMBE represents academic institutions, private industry, and professional engineering societies.

American Society of Agricultural and Biological Engineers (ASABE)
2950 Niles Rd.
St. Joseph, MI 49085
phone: (800) 371-2723
fax: (269) 429-3852
e-mail: hq@asabe.org
website: www.asabe.org

The ASABE has been the professional home of engineers and others worldwide who endeavor to find sustainable solutions for an ever growing population. This member-driven technical and educational organization provides networking, publications, and student scholarships and awards.

Biomedical Engineering Society (BMES)
8201 Corporate Dr., Suite 1125
Landover, MD 20785-2224
phone: (301) 459-1999; toll-free: (877) 871-2637
fax: (301) 459-2444
website: www.bmes.org

The goal of the BMES is to serve as the world's leading society of professionals devoted to developing and using engineering and technology to advance human health and well-being. The BMES also supports student chapters throughout the United States. It has a commitment to student learning and posts several educational videos on its website.

National Institute of Biomedical Imaging and Bioengineering (NIBIB)
National Institutes of Health
9000 Rockville Pike
Bethesda, MD 20892
phone: (301) 496-4000
website: www.nih.gov

The mission of the NIBIB is to improve health by leading the development and accelerating the application of biomedical technologies. The institute is committed to integrating the physical and engineering sciences with the life sciences to advance basic research and medical care. It offers grants and educational opportunities to those in the field.

Society for Biological Engineering (SBE)
120 Wall St., 23rd Floor
New York, NY 10005-4020
phone: (800) 242-4363
website: www.aiche.org

The SBE is a global organization of leading engineers and scientists dedicated to advancing the integration of biology with engineering. The SBE promotes the integration of biology with engineering and realizes its benefits through bioprocessing, biomedical, and biomolecular applications.

Microbiologist

What Does a Microbiologist Do?

Microbiologists work in a variety of different settings and in a variety of different capacities. They work in the food industry, in agriculture, in pharmaceuticals, and the health field. They work everywhere the study of microorganisms is important. Some microbiologists are bacteriologists, focusing on the study of bacteria. Those who study viruses are called virologists. Mycologists study fungi. Immunologists study the immune system.

Microbiologists in the health care field use their knowledge in the study of disease. For example, microbiologists may study microorganisms that cause disease and use their findings to help develop a vaccine or new treatment drug. As part of this research microbiologists often maintain cultures of bacteria or other microorganisms. They may also collect specimens of microorganisms for further study. Connor Bamford, a PhD microbiology student in Ireland, describes his typical day on microbiology careers.org.uk:

At a Glance:
Microbiologist

Minimum Educational Requirements
Bachelor's degree in microbiology

Personal Qualities
Analytical; good at math and science; good written and verbal communication skills

Certification and Licensing
Optional

Working Conditions
Indoors in a laboratory setting; some outdoor work may be required

Salary Range
About $39,720 to $117,690

Number of Jobs
20,100 in 2012

Future Job Outlook
Seven percent increase through 2022

From when I arrive in the morning, my time is mostly taken up with me being in the lab working with DNA and bacteria, or then moving into tissue culture where I am working with, and taking care of, our cell lines and viruses. I'll usually plan what experiments I have to carry out the previous day and then I can just get down to the work yet the most time-consuming aspect is sitting down and looking through the data you get back. This is mostly done with copious amounts of caffeine. During coffee breaks—or that 15 minutes I get for lunch—I will try and make myself read what new papers have been published in my field.

Microbiologists also work in jobs that deal with energy and the environment. The development of microbes that eat oil that has spilled in the ocean, for example, came about as a result of the work of microbiologists. Microbiologists also work to develop clean energy by studying how to use microbes to break down waste. They also are involved in research on climate change through the study of how microbes react to environmental temperature fluctuations. Microbiologists who work in agriculture study harmful and beneficial microbes in the soil. One goal of this work is to use beneficial microbes to fight pests and plant diseases. They also study the diseases that plague farm animals.

Another increasingly popular area of interest for microbiologists is forensic science. Law enforcement agencies employ microbiologists, who use molecular biology techniques to help solve crimes.

The work of microbiologists affects everyday life. For example, they play a role in food safety, making sure that food that is sold does not contain harmful microbes that can make people sick. They also develop microbes that are needed for making foods such as cheese, yogurt, beer, and wine. The study of microbes has even influenced sports clothing. Some sports clothing contains silver because it has been shown to fight the microbes that react to sweat that leaves body odor on clothing.

No matter which field microbiologists work in, they use computers and laboratory instruments and often share their research with other scientists. Powerful electron microscopes allow microbiologists to closely examine microorganisms, and computers help keep track of and analyze the large amounts of data collected. Research methods and findings are usually communicated to others in the form of papers or journal articles and oral presentations. In addition to sharing their own research, microbiologists are expected to keep up with the latest research from other scientists.

A recent survey of research completed by microbiologists, taken from issues of *Science Daily*, reveals the diversity of this unique field:

- By studying certain bacteria in the mouth, microbiologists are finding a link with heart valve disease.
- By studying bacteria in the oceans, microbiologists are finding a greater diversity of healthy bacteria in ocean water frequented by bathers.
- Microbiologists have discovered that planting maize in soil contaminated by the heavy metals of former mine sites helps decrease the pollution and bacteria in the soil.
- Study of chicken served in hospitals found that 85 percent was contaminated by harmful bacteria. Microbiologists recommended safe meat handling procedures to reduce the levels.
- Microbiologists are mapping indoor biodiversity and finding that buildings contain identifiable microbial signatures of their human inhabitants. They are hoping to use the information to improve home health and safety.

And this list represents just a small sampling of the unique and divergent work of a microbiologist.

How Do You Become a Microbiologist?

Education

The minimum requirement for a microbiologist is a bachelor's degree, but most have higher degrees. High school students who are interested in a microbiology career should take classes such as chemistry, biology, microbiology, and immunology (if available). Most microbiologists who head up research projects have attained or are working toward a PhD. Microbiology PhD candidate

Christopher Allen, interviewed on the University of Texas website gsbsumtb.edu says:

> My interest in graduate school began while taking a general microbiology course during my junior year of college. . . . As the semester progressed, I found myself increasingly fascinated with this particular field, especially in the areas of environmental and clinical microbiology. . . . Upon completion of my Bachelor of Science degree, I pursued a Master's degree continuing my work in environmental microbiology. I used this time to decide if I wanted to seriously pursue a career in research and eventually decided to proceed on this course. My decision was to continue in the field of microbiology, but my growing interest in infectious disease research impacted my decision to pursue a Ph.D in clinical microbiology.

Kelley Madden used his microbiology degree to get a job with a brewery. On google.com he speaks about the type of coursework that helped him achieve his career goal of becoming a microbiologist for a brewery. "Kids in college have the opportunity to take more specific classes like Fermentation Science, Food Science and Brewing. There are also brewing specific universities. If you continue to be interested in the brewing industry I would highly recommend going to a school that offers these types of classes."

Certification and Licensing

Although certification is not mandatory, some organizations offer exams to qualify a microbiologist to work in a certain industry. For example, the National Registry of Certified Microbiologists (NRCM) certifies professional microbiologists at the bachelor's, master's, and doctorate levels in food safety and quality, pharmaceutical and medical devices, and biological safety. The American Board of Medical Microbiology is a certification program for those involved in the medical field. The American College of Microbiology offers certification to microbiologists and immunologists and works with accrediting postdoctoral training programs. Other organizations certify microbiologists in other areas such as public health or the study of pathogens.

Volunteer Work and Internships

Many microbiologists state that practical experience is essential and internships are a great way to gain experience in the field. Individual colleges and universities offer internships for their students, but organizations such as the National Science Foundation and the National Institutes of Health offer over a hundred highly sought-after internships to microbiology students.

Skills and Personality

Microbiologists require a strong interest in science, particularly the fields of chemistry, biochemistry, and genetics. Since microbiology is a field dominated by research, a person interested in a career in this field needs to have excellent analytical and interpretive skills, be detail minded, observant, and determined. They must be willing to spend much of their time gathering and interpreting the results of their experiments. They must extrapolate from those experiments the final results to use in the applications of their research. They must be able to work on a team and communicate well with others, both in writing and speaking. On mygradspace.wordpress.com graduate student Lisa Burnett describes how she became interested in microbiology.

> I have always been interested in science in general, particularly the general fields of Biology and Medicine. I also love to "solve the puzzle" and was never satisfied with just knowing a fact; I always needed to know why. I was first introduced to Microbiology in 10th grade when I was allowed to substitute that for a semester of general Biology. I dove into it with everything I had (mainly because I was younger than everyone else in the class and felt I had something to prove) and came away from that class with a very strong love for the topic and a respect for the power of the microbe.

One of the most important characteristics for anyone thinking of becoming a microbiologist is perseverance, says Bamford, whose comments appear on microbiologycareers.org.uk. Scientific research does not always go smoothly. He says, "Firstly: it's not always going to work the first time, nor the second (maybe not the third) but keep at it and eventually you will get there—determination is very important in science. And secondly: keep reading. All the information and ideas may already be in the science literature, you've just got to find them."

Bamford also notes the importance of a passion for science: "I used to believe that the only reason I was doing this was because I was good at science in school and university, but I've come to realise that I have always been a bit into science my whole life, what with dinosaurs, fossils and chemistry. I guess if you couple a somewhat geeky school kid who has a passion for science with good teachers and mentors, you'll get a potential research scientist."

On the Job

Employers

Since the field of microbiology is vast, the number of employers is equally large and varied. According to the Bureau of Labor Statistics, the industries that employed the most microbiologists in 2012 were pharmaceutical and medicine manufacturing, 23 percent; research and development in the physical, engineering, and life sciences, 23 percent; federal government, excluding postal service, 14 percent; state and local government, excluding education and hospitals, 11 percent; and colleges, universities, and professional schools, 9 percent.

Working Conditions

Most microbiologists work in a lab setting and typically keep regular hours. According to the Bureau of Labor Statistics, some microbiologists have to collect samples of soil, seawater, and other substances that contain microorganisms. Some microbiologists spend part of their time in classrooms and offices. Those who work in universities and other research centers may have flexible hours, but their work weeks generally total more than forty hours. Some overtime or shift work may be necessary when a project must be completed, or when an experiment must be monitored around the clock. Microbiologists can work independently or as part of a team.

Earnings

According to the Bureau of Labor Statistics , the median annual wage for microbiologists was $66,260 in May 2012. The lowest 10 percent earned less than $39,720, and the top 10 percent earned more than $117,690. The BLS says that pay varies depending on the industry a microbiologist works in. Typical pay for federal jobs is $96,520; for pharmaceutical and medicine manufacturing, $67,070; for research and development in the physical, engineering, and life sciences, $62,920; for jobs in state and local government (excluding education and hospitals), $54,640; for colleges, universities, and professional schools, $52,790.

Opportunities for Advancement

Career advancement for microbiologists is typically tied to level of education. Those with bachelor's degrees have limited opportunities, while those with PhDs will be offered opportunities to head up research experiments as a project manager or research lead.

What Is the Future Outlook for Microbiologists?

According to the Bureau of Labor Statistics, employment of microbiologists is projected to grow 7 percent through 2022. Because of the sheer variety of jobs, microbiologists will continue to be needed in research to help develop new medicines and treatments, food producers will need microbiologists to test for food safety and to develop new ways of growing foods, and energy companies will employ microbiologists to develop new energy sources.

Find Out More

American Dairy Science Association (ADSA)
1111 N. Dunlap Ave.
Savoy, IL 61874
phone: (217) 356-5146; fax: (217) 398-4119
e-mail: adsa@assochq
website: www.adsa.org

The ADSA is an international organization of educators, scientists, and industry representatives of the dairy industry. Microbiologists who are involved in food science, including cheesemaking, yogurt making, and other cultured dairy products, are members of this organization.

American Society for Microbiology (ASM)
1752 N St. NW
Washington, DC 20036-2904
phone: (202) 737-3600
website: www.asm.org

The ASM is the world's largest scientific society of individuals interested in the microbiological sciences. The group's mission is to advance the microbiological sciences as a vehicle for understanding life processes and to apply and communicate this knowledge for the improvement of health and environmental and economic well-being worldwide.

Institute of Food Technologists (IFT)
525 W. Van Buren, Suite 1000
Chicago, IL 60607
phone: (312) 782-8424; fax: (312) 782-8348
e-mail: info@ift.org
website: www.ift.org

The Institute of Food Technologists exists to advance the science of food. The IFT's long-range vision is to ensure a safe and abundant food supply contributing to healthier people everywhere.

Society for Industrial Microbiology and Biotechnology (SIMB)
3929 Old Lee Hwy., Suite 92A
Fairfax, VA 22030-2421
phone: (703) 691-3357; fax: (703) 691-7991
e-mail: simbhq@simbhq.org
website: www.simbhq.org

The SIMB is dedicated to the advancement of microbiological sciences, especially as they apply to industrial products, biotechnology, materials, and processes. SIMB promotes the exchange of scientific information through its meetings and publications, and serves as liaison among the specialized fields of microbiology.

Biofuels Developer

What Does a Biofuels Developer Do?

Biofuels developers create alternatives to fossil fuels. Biofuels are energy that is made from living matter—mostly plants. Bioethanol, biodiesel, and biogas are common types of biofuels, and although they currently have many uses developers are constantly searching for new and better ways to produce these and other types of biofuels. A biofuels developer's work always involves chemistry—how to eke out the most from each fuel and fuel mixture. For example, bioethanol, a familiar biofuel, usually consists of a blend of gasoline and alcohol made from corn, sorghum, potatoes, wheat, sugar cane, or biomass. Biomass is living matter left over from harvesting another crop, such as cornstalks or other vegetable waste. Biofuels developers research different crops to see which of these various blends and in what measure will burn at the right temperature, burn cleanly, and burn well enough to get reasonable mileage and performance.

Other fuels that have been developed or are currently being worked on by biofuels developers include biodiesel, which is

At a Glance:
Biofuels Developer

Minimum Educational Requirements

Bachelor's degree in chemistry, biochemistry, microbiology, chemical engineering, or related field

Personal Qualities

Innovative, perceptive, insightful, highly analytical, excellent oral and written communication

Certification and Licensing

None

Working Conditions

Indoors in an office or lab environment

Salary Range

About $96,000 to $144,000

Number of Jobs

As of 2012 about 170,000

Future Job Outlook

7 to 13 percent growth through 2022

produced from oil taken from plants or animals. It is currently mostly blended with petroleum diesel. Grease or oil from cooking can also be converted to biodiesel and is more sustainable because it is a by-product of another process. Currently, with existing engines these oils can make up only 20 percent of the vehicle's fuel mixture. Developers are trying to find the right mix of oils so that the fuel burns cleanly enough to meet Environmental Protection Agency (EPA) and California emission standards set in 2007 for diesel. Gerhard Knothe is a research chemist and biofuels developer at the Food and Industrial Oil Research unit of the US Department of Agriculture's National Center for Agricultural Utilization Research in Peoria, Illinois. His interview appears on ScienceWatch.com: "My research is mainly concerned with the use of vegetable oils and their derivatives as alternative diesel fuels and related aspects. My educational background is in chemistry, specifically a Ph.D. in organic polymer chemistry."

The last biofuel, biogas, is created as a by-product of decomposing plant and animal waste such as landfills, waste treatment facilities, and dairies. Biogas consists primarily of methane and carbon dioxide, both of which are greenhouse gases. The main challenge for biofuels developers is to make sure biogas burns cleanly to avoid having these by-products pollute the atmosphere. However, this fuel holds a lot of promise for developing countries because it has other uses besides transportation. Biogas can also be used for cooking and electricity and can be developed from readily found materials such as animal dung. Some biogas developers teach people in countries such as India to make biogas. The United States also takes advantage of biogas. Freshkills landfill in New York City produces enough biogas to power thirty thousand homes a year.

A biofuels developer may have a background in chemistry or biology but also needs math to do his or her work. This is because much of developing a new fuel depends on calculating the amount of raw product it will take to produce enough fuel to run a generator, electric light, or car. A biofuels developer who is in charge of a scientific team needs to oversee and communicate to others on staff. Biofuels developers also need to communicate the results of their research to their supervisors.

Much technical skill is involved in researching the biofuels. Developers must understand the potential of a particular fuel source, such as algae, then know how to separate and recover the fuel from

A researcher works with beakers containing algae that will be used in the production of biofuels. Biofuels developers seek to improve existing alternative fuels as well as create new ones.

the source. Then they have to evaluate the efficiency of the fuel and the cost efficiency of extracting the fuel. They must set up and construct their own experiments to figure out the viability of the fuel source. For this reason biofuels developers are not entry-level jobs but usually the culmination of years in the field.

Often biofuels developers work closely with farmers. In 2014, for example, biofuels developers were working with North Dakota farmers to develop a new type of ethanol from sugar beets. Because farmers must plan their crops three to four years in advance, biofuel developers must guarantee farmers that they will take all of their beets for several years in a row while they are developing the fuel. The beets that produce biofuels are called industrial beets, and they are genetically different from the beets grown for humans to eat. In addition to obtaining enough beets to make a refinery economically efficient, crops for biofuels must meet certain Environmental Protection Agency standards to reduce greenhouse gas emissions. So biofuel developers must prove that their fuel, still under development, will be able to do so. There will be other hurdles once they have obtained the beets and built a refinery to extract the sugars and further refine those sugars into a usable fuel. All of these steps will be overseen by the biofuels developer.

Because the federal government oversees and often provides financial incentives to biofuels companies, people who work in biofuel development have to be able to work with many restrictions. Biofuel companies also work with the federal government in an attempt to influence energy policy, including relaxing or implementing different fuel standards or changing standards that may be outdated as a result of new fuel developments. Biofuels developers, because they are the experts on the impact of their fuels, are often asked to participate in these discussions. Susan Hager was a biologist working on cancer treatments who switched to working in the biofuels industry. She comments on these difficulties in an interview in biomassmagazine.com: "I really thought, what could be more challenging than working with [the] FDA trying to get drugs approved and on the market? . . . Trying to establish consistent energy policy is actually harder than getting a cancer drug approved."

Another large project involving the work of biofuels developers is a collaboration between the Boeing Company, an Abu Dhabi airline company, and others. Biofuel developers at Boeing are working on a new type of biofuel from a plant called a halophyte. These plants have several advantages because they can be grown in the desert so the crops will not compete with food crops. They can also be watered with saltwater, so will not use up valuable freshwater supplies. Using halophytes to develop a biodiesel could have a significant impact on lowering the cost of fuel. Boeing and other airline companies are interested in developing biofuels because the cost of fuel has a significant impact on the cost of travel.

How Do You Become a Biofuels Developer?

Education

The minimum education required for this position is a bachelor's degree in chemistry, biochemistry, microbiology, chemical engineering, or related field. However, most employers will require that a job candidate have at least five to ten years of experience in the biofuels field in addition to a bachelor's degree. Those with a master's degree, however, will be not be required to have as much job experience. Candidates who go on to have earned a PhD degree may be able to have little or no actual work experience and still be hired for an entry-level position. This is because the position of developer often carries with it managerial responsibilities and knowledge of specialized equipment.

Volunteer Work and Internships

As with many jobs that require lab work, many in the field highly recommend working an internship to gain valuable work experience. Interested students can seek out internships at companies that specialize in biofuels and also at oil companies, which are doing their own biofuels research. Most of the internship opportunities are for graduate students. One internship offered at the National Renewable Energy Laboratory posted on Indeed.com describes the internship duties this way: "The intern will join a team of researchers who perform environmental sustainability assessments of energy technologies. The specific project involves estimating air pollutant emissions from the life cycle of biofuel production (feedstock production, handling and transport, fuel conversion). The core skills required are centered on chemical or process engineering–based estimation of air emissions from industrial processes, focused mainly at the biorefinery."

Skills and Personality

A biofuels developer uses many of the same skills that apply in other science careers. That is why a variety of different science degrees can be used to become a biofuels developer. Often, though, a desire to do work that benefits Earth is something biofuels developers share. In an interview for biomassmagazine.com Hager talks about what led her to switch from immunology and cancer research to a career in biofuels. "The clean energy sector is probably the only other industry as altruistic as trying to cure cancer. . . . I started to get passionate about the technologies I was reading about. The company I joined had this really cool bacteria—biology at the core with really slick engineering." People who work in this industry often have an interest in the environment and like the idea of searching for innovative ways to address environmental concerns.

In addition to having an interest in a green job, other skills are required. Excellent written and oral communication skills are necessary, as research is often written up and must be communicated to others. Knowledge of federal regulations and requirements of the development of biofuels is also necessary. As with many science-based careers, biofuels developers will also work with a lot of technical equipment, including oxygen monitors, flow sensors, compound microscopes, mass spectrometers, as well as technical software.

On the Job

Employers

A variety of entities are involved in the development of biofuels. The federal government, colleges and universities, large oil companies such as BP, and airline companies such as Boeing are all potential employers of biofuels developers. There are also companies dedicated to the development of biofuels. One such company is Algae Systems, which is focusing on the development of fuel from algae. American Standard Renewable Fuel Corporation is another example; this company works specifically with the development and use of fuel from landfills. The website advancedbiofuelsusa.info lists hundreds of US and foreign companies working in biofuels development.

Working Conditions

Biofuel developers usually work indoors in a lab or office environment. They must use specialized equipment and be proficient at using scientific instruments and lab protocol to come up with accurate research results. Those who work in colleges and universities may have a grant to complete their work.

Earnings

According to recruiter.com, biofuels developers earn a high salary, from $96,000 to $144,000. This is tied to the fact that the job requires either an advanced degree or an undergraduate degree with the addition of at least five to ten years of work experience.

Opportunities for Advancement

The position of biofuels developer is usually already at a management level position, and so opportunities to advance beyond it are few. However, running a research and development project is the epitome of advancement in this position. In such a position, a biofuels developer is involved with a product from conception in a lab all the way through to a commercial product.

What Is the Future Outlook for Biofuels Developer?

The Bureau of Labor Statistics, while not offering hard numbers, believes that all areas of green jobs will grow. The bureau is optimistic about careers in biofuels in particular because of the increase in government and private investment in the efforts. Careers in biofuels, in particular specialized positions such as in product development, should continue to experience robust growth.

Find Out More

Advanced Biofuels USA
507 N. Bentz St.
Frederick, MD 21701
phone: (301) 644-1395
website: advancedbiofuelsusa.info

Advanced Biofuels USA promotes research, development, and improvement of advanced biofuels technologies, production, marketing, and delivery through sustainable development, cultivation, and processing of advanced biofuels crops and agricultural and forestry residues and wastes.

Algae Biomass Organization (ABO)
125 St. Paul St.
PO Box 369

Preston, MN 55965-0369
phone: (877) 531-5512
website: algaebiomass.org

ABO is a nonprofit organization whose mission is to promote the development of viable commercial markets for renewable and sustainable commodities derived from algae.

Biotechnology Industry Organization (BIO)
1201 Maryland Ave. SW, Suite 900
Washington, DC 20024
phone: (202) 962-9200
website: bio.org

BIO is the world's largest trade association representing biotechnology companies, academic institutions, state biotechnology centers, and related organizations across the United States and in more than thirty other nations. BIO members are involved in the research and development of innovative health care, agricultural, industrial, and environmental biotechnology products.

Clean Fuels Development Coalition (CFDC)
4641 Montgomery Ave., Suite 350
Bethesda, MD 20814
phone: (301) 718-0077
website: cleanfuelsdc.org

The CFDC actively supports the increased production and use of fuels that can reduce air pollution and oil imports. CFDC develops support in industry and government to foster a healthy national energy policy. CFDC works with all interested parties to support clean fuel regulations and new technologies.

Biological Technician

Biological technicians work in a variety of fields, all involving the study of living organisms. They may assist biologists and microbiologists with laboratory tests and experiments or work for pharmaceutical companies helping with the development of drugs. Others work in mining and industrial production analyzing ore reserves. Some biological technicians are involved in testing samples for environmental impact studies. These studies are required for some construction projects. Others work for government agencies in wildlife resource management analyzing wildlife populations.

As valuable assistants, technicians set up, operate, and maintain laboratory instruments; they keep tabs on the experiments going on in the lab, making observations, recording the results, and offering opinions on results. The biological technician's responsibilities have grown more complex and varied with the development of new technologies and instrumentation. They have become experts at maintaining

At a Glance:

Biological Technician

Minimum Educational Requirements

Bachelor's degree in biology

Personal Qualities

Analytical, good observational and critical thinking skills; technology-minded; good oral and written communication

Certification and Licensing

Depending on the type of work, some states and government institutions require certification

Working Conditions

Indoors in lab conditions; some fieldwork may be required

Salary Range

About $25,280 to $64,880

Number of Jobs

As of 2012 about 80,200

Future Job Outlook

Ten percent growth through 2022

and adjusting lab equipment in order to produce the best results. With robots performing many of the tasks that technicians used to do, they are more involved in using computers to monitor experiments. They are also the professionals who maintain detailed logs to record their actions in order to retrace exactly how they prepared and maintained lab experiments. They may also be involved in quality control and testing drugs to make sure that the drug's ingredients are pure and in the right proportions of strength and durability.

A list of the complex machinery a biological technician often interacts with and maintains is daunting. It includes:

- DNA sequence analyzers.
- Manual or electronic hematology differential cell counters for analyzing blood.
- Robotic or automated liquid handling systems to increase the exactitude of lab experiments.
- Spectrofluorimeters or fluorimeters to analyze samples of bodily fluids.
- Temperature cycling chambers or thermal cyclers to maintain or change temperatures in experiments.

In addition, biological technicians may work with a variety of different types of computer software. This may include analytical or scientific software, database user interface and query software, graphics or photo imaging software, spreadsheet software, and word processing software.

For biological technicians technical expertise is often as important as scientific knowledge. Joel works for the National Institutes of Health as a biological technician. Part of his job is to maintain a library of DNA information. He also maintains the lab instruments used in collecting the DNA information. He describes his typical workday on allhealthcare.com.

My typical workday involves constructing deoxyribonucleic acid (or DNA) libraries and serving as a team leader for the National Intramural Sequencing Center (NISC) library construction group. A DNA library is made by breaking up a

DNA sample into smaller units for further studies. My work of constructing DNA libraries is the same as my colleagues in the group.

My technical specialty is DNA fingerprinting, a laboratory procedure that helps us correctly identify and track the DNA samples we process. The results look like a bar code that retail stores use to scan purchases. It serves a similar purpose too. The DNA sequence of any individual is unique. So a DNA fingerprint is like a personalized bar code. I compare the DNA fingerprints of the samples we process to the reference fingerprints made by the lab that sent us the samples. If the DNA "bar codes" match-up, then we know we have the right sample. We use a special software program (LINS) that helps us compare the two samples. It also helps us track every step in the DNA processing.

Joel's experience epitomizes the role of the biological technician involved in the day-to-day running of a laboratory as well as keeping track of experiments and maintaining equipment.

Some biological technicians work in agriculture. These technicians work with plant and animal experiments. They may be required to record the data that such experiments produce and also perform the daily care of the animals used in the research. In experiments of new lines of plant seeds they may be required to plant the new seeds in a specific area to see which seeds are germinating and where and to collect samples of plants for further testing. Biological technicians can also be involved in maintaining experimental data on agricultural plant and animal diseases. In this capacity they can be involved in the study of parasites and other harmful insects. They study different insects, their life cycle, and their negative effects on the environment. They identify ways of controlling insect growth and methods to cure the diseases they spread.

Other biological technicians work in the field of energy alternatives, such as biofuels. As in other areas, these technicians aid in the data gathering, experiments, and maintaining of equipment used in the field. They may be involved, for example, in crunching data on a particular energy alternative, such as a new biofuel, to measure and rate the new biofuel against an existing fuel to help determine its efficacy and economic viability. Some biological technicians work in the food science industry. They can work for the government inspecting and analyzing food samples, or work in the private sector in the same capacity. They may be involved in analyzing chemicals and additives in food. They analyze these ingredients and their use in food products to make sure that such products are safe for people and animals.

They can work in quality control, to ensure that food products meet the company's and government standards. They may also be involved in the development of new food. A cereal company for example, would use a biological technician to evaluate ingredients for a new cereal.

How Do You Become a Biological Technician?

Education

A bachelor's degree in biology or another science-related field is the minimum requirement for biological technicians. Most colleges and universities offer bachelor's degree programs in the biological sciences. In these programs students typically take courses in biology, ecology, microbiology, and physiology. These courses in particular usually require laboratory work, which is an essential part of the biological technician's job. They must also take courses in chemistry, mathematics, physics, and computer science to help them maintain and calibrate the laboratory equipment they use. Many community colleges offer technician training as part of a bachelor's or master's degree program, especially in fields such as biomanufacturing. There are thirty-two such programs in California alone.

Biological technician Peggy Hall started out not knowing what kind of work she wanted to do. She describes her education on nihlifeworks.com:

> I chose to become a biological technician by accident. In high school, I did not do that well in biology. When I went to college, I was thinking of nursing as a major. After taking biology in college, I was doing better and liked the course. At the same time, I was volunteering in a hospital as a nursing-clerical as-

sistant. With time, I realized that I didn't like the environment. It just didn't fit my personality. The definitive moment came one night when a lady came up to me and just kept repeating the word "help." I didn't know what to do. I couldn't help her. It was an upsetting moment. That's when I decided to choose biology as a major. I was performing well in my science classes and my interest in biology kept growing.

Certification and Licensing

Many employers prefer applicants who are certified by a recognized professional association, and some states and public hospitals require certification in order to work in their labs. Information on licensure is available from state departments of health or boards of occupational licensing. Which certification to obtain depends on the specialty of the biological technician. For example, medical technologists, a subset of biological technician, can be certified through the American Medical Technologists organization. The American Society of Clinical Pathologists offers a certification program that is quite thorough. The certification requires that candidates pass a written exam and complete a fifty-week US military medical course.

Volunteer Work and Internships

Internships are readily available for those studying to become biological technicians. Many employers encourage students to take a semester off to work in a laboratory to gain practical experience before they graduate. Companies and government agencies offer many other internships during the summer. Just one listing for an internship as a biological technician in wildlife studies for the Southwest Conservation Corps reveals that such internships yield real work. The duties include: "Survey, maps, and documents of a variety of wildlife species and habitat conditions including populations, vegetation surveys, boundaries, rare and endangered species habitat; compile and organize survey data in current files and other sources; prepare narratives, and reports on and overlays of areas surveyed; identify from inventories areas which meet established criteria that would benefit from habitat improvement and/or expansion efforts."

Skills and Personality

Though the role of biological technicians is one of support, the knowledge and skills required are highly technical and varied. These technicians must be science oriented and understand and have an academic background in biology, chemistry, and mathematics. In addition, because writing and communicating is a large part of the job, they must have excellent written and verbal communication skills. They must also be good at analysis, including the ability to think critically, analyze and interpret data, and be quick to solve problems or adapt to new knowledge if the research they are working on is showing different results than expected.

On the Job

Employers

Biological technicians work for the government, colleges, and universities and in many areas of the private sector including medical and agricultural research labs, pharmaceutical companies, chemical companies, food processing and food development companies, and scientific firms, such as those involved in DNA sequencing. According to the Bureau of Labor Statistics, biological technicians worked in the following areas in 2012: Colleges, universities, and professional schools employed 19,770 technicians; 18,640 were employed in scientific research and development services; 10,960 were employed in the federal executive branch; 6,420 were employed in pharmaceutical and medicine manufacturing; and 3,560 were employed in general medical and surgical hospitals.

States with the most need for biological technicians are ones that also have large technical industries and research schools and laboratories. These states include California, Massachusetts, Pennsylvania, Maryland, and New York.

Working Conditions

Most biological technicians work indoors in a laboratory setting. They must be well versed in keeping a sterile, contaminant-free workspace in order to maintain the best environment for research.

Earnings

According to the Bureau of Labor Statistics, the median annual wage for biological technicians was $39,750 in 2012. The lowest 10 percent earned less than $25,280, and the top 10 percent earned more than $64,880. The BLS breaks down salary for biological technicians by industry: chemical manufacturing, $45,380; research and development in the physical, engineering, and life sciences, $42,330; colleges, universities, and professional schools, $40,450; hospitals, $38,450; testing laboratories, $36,260; and federal agencies, $33,630.

Opportunities for Advancement

Opportunities for advancement for biological technicians can be obtained by pursuing jobs in industries that pay higher wages, such as chemical manufacturing or academic research, and by developing expertise in various technologies and software.

What Is the Future Outlook for Biological Technicians?

According to the Bureau of Labor Statistics, employment of biological technicians is expected to grow by 10 percent through 2022. The BLS sees demand for the profession increasing because of food, environmental, and medical industries requiring more biological research. The search for treatments for diseases such as cancer and Alzheimer's is likely to lead to increased need for biological technicians. In addition, the agriculture industry will require more technicians as it seeks to develop genetically engineered crops and find ways to increase yields while protecting the environment. Finally, technicians will be needed in the search for energy alternatives, including biofuels.

Find Out More

American Society for Biochemistry and Molecular Biology (ASBMB)
11200 Rockville Pike, Suite 302
Rockville, MD 20852-3110

phone: (240) 283-6600
website: www.asbmb.org

The ASBMB is a nonprofit scientific and educational organization. Its purpose is to advance the science of biochemistry and molecular biology through publication of several scientific and educational journals and by organizing scientific meetings, advocating for funding of basic research and education, and supporting of science education at all levels.

American Society for Microbiology (ASM)
1752 N St. NW
Washington, DC 20036-2904
phone: (202) 737-3600
website: www.asm.org

The ASM is the world's largest scientific society of individuals interested in the microbiological sciences. The mission of the American Society for Microbiology is to advance the microbiological sciences as a vehicle for understanding life processes and to apply and communicate this knowledge for the improvement of health and environmental and economic well-being worldwide.

American Society for Nutrition (ASN)
9650 Rockville Pike
Bethesda, MD 20814
phone: (301) 634-7050
website: www.nutrition.org

The ASN is a nonprofit organization dedicated to bringing together the world's top researchers, clinical nutritionists, and industry to advance our knowledge and application of nutrition for the sake of humans and animals.

American Society of Human Genetics (ASHG)
9650 Rockville Pike
Bethesda, MD 20814
phone: (866) 486-4363
website: www.ashg.org

The ASHG is the primary professional membership organization for human genetics specialists worldwide. The society's members include researchers, academicians, clinicians, laboratory practice professionals, genetic counselors, nurses, and others who have a special interest in the field of human genetics. It publishes *The American Journal of Human Genetics*.

Bioinformatics Specialist

What Does a Bioinformatics Specialist Do?

The field of bioinformatics is relatively new. Bioinformatics basically refers to using information technology (IT) in the study of proteins and genes. Bioinformatics is part of the realm of information management. Scientists have begun to use computers and software to process, sort, reconfigure, and analyze the reams of data on biological processes they generate during their research. Computers are being adapted to quickly process and understand biological and chemical processes. A person who has experience in computers and software and knowledge of biology, especially how it relates to drug development, will find this emerging field particularly wide open.

Bioinformatics specialists use computer software and hardware to collect, manage, and study biological and biochemical data at a molecular level. They design computer databases and develop mathematical formulas, called al-

At a Glance:

Bioinformatics Specialist

Minimum Educational Requirements
Bachelor's degree, though many positions require a master's degree or PhD

Personal Qualities
Strong technology and math skills, interest in computers and software

Certification and Licensing
None

Working Conditions
Indoors in a laboratory

Salary Range
About $25,000 to $100,000+

Future Job Outlook
Expected to grow 3 to 9 percent through 2020

gorithms, to study and manage this data. For example, they may use an algorithm to search for a particular DNA or amino acid sequence in databases. When a new protein is identified, a bioinformatics specialist might help identify what family of proteins it belongs to, where the protein is located in the cell, what the protein's potential function is, what biological cell process it might participate in, its gene profile in diseased versus healthy tissue and in various organs in the body, and what class of drugs may be able to target it if it causes illness. Bioinformatics specialists may also be called bioinformaticists, bioinformatics scientists, biometricians, biostatisticians, or computational biologists. No matter what they are called, or which field they work in, their job involves information management.

Bioinformatics specialists usually work in one of three fields. They may specialize in genomics, the study of genes; health informatics, specializing in the health care field; or the physical sciences, in which they work with medical equipment—maintaining, reconfiguring, and developing new software.

In explaining the importance of the bioinformatics specialist on bioteach.ubc.ca, biology bioinformatics expert Ryan Brinkman from Xenon Genetics in Vancouver, Canada, says that they use computers

> to help understand biology. Of course it is more than just putting data into a spreadsheet and making a pretty graph. I think the real push for bioinformatics started when biologists started getting really large datasets; the kind that no longer fits well into a spreadsheet. What biologists needed were people who understood databases, and how to put data in, and more importantly get data out, so we can answer those questions that we are trying to answer. This led to the development and exponential growth of databases like GenBank. So by extension, I would say most of bioinformatics is using computers to understand or process large biological datasets that are probably sitting in some sort of database.

How Do You Become a Bioinformatics Specialist?

Education

While some entry level work can be obtained with a bachelor's degree in biology or computer science, most bioinformatics specialist jobs require a master's degree or a PhD. This is because it takes time to become well versed in both biology and the computer skills required. Brinkman explains how difficult it was for him to decide on the career and the degrees he needed to obtain before he was finally able to get the job he loved:

> It wasn't until I started doing bioinformatics that I finally knew what I wanted to do in my life. It wasn't something that I set out to learn, or had heard about. I did my undergraduate degree in Biology and Biotechnology (even that took me the first few years of undergrad to figure out), but I was also something of a proto-geek. That is I liked messing about with computers, but I hadn't taken any classes or anything like that. My first real job out of undergrad was designing databases for a group of molecular biologists, but from there I was pointed to a job at the Genome Sequencing Center of St. Louis. This was ten years ago, and I think the job description was Scientific Programmer, but what I really was doing was bioinformatics. After doing that for a few years I knew I had found my true calling, but that I also wanted to do more interesting things [than] what I was doing, so I went back to school to get my Ph.D. in genetics and after that I was lucky enough to find the perfect job at Xenon which lets me do really interesting science, and get paid for it. I was motivated to get into bioinformatics because I found that I loved what I was doing. Everything is new, so there is no wrong way to do something because people haven't found the right way yet. That and one of the wonderful things about being a scientist is the feeling of discovery. As a bioinformatician you get first crack at the data that the biologist worked so hard to generate.

Volunteer Work and Internships

As with many science careers, those in the field recommend obtaining lab experience as soon as possible. Just a scan of internship possibilities for undergraduates and graduates in bioinformatics yields a variety of results from a number of companies and universities including the National Marrow Donor Program, Dow Industries, and the Fred Hutchinson Cancer Research Center. Some colleges and universities that offer bioinformatics programs also can recommend internships for students.

Skills and Personality

Because the bioinformatics field is truly an intersection of a number of different disciplines, students who pursue this career must have a number of interests and spend a great deal of time on their education. Ultimately, bioinformatics specialists must have knowledge of biology and of computer science. Successful bioinformatics specialists must be able to communicate knowledgeably in both areas. A person talented in computer science, for example, must be able to communicate to biologists on the topic of the research they are involved in and what the computer can and cannot do to be of assistance. Students pursuing this field must be analytical problem solvers with great critical thinking skills. They must also be good communicators, as they must be able to work in teams and explain their methodology and their results. They may also be called upon to write and publish research papers. In addition, they must also be detail oriented and have patience and perseverance, as rewriting software to produce certain algorithms for research is time-consuming and has many moments of trial and error.

Anne Condon, professor of computer science at the University of British Columbia and a bioinformatics specialist offers her advice on the requirements of this career. Condon's interview appears on bioteach .ubc.ca:

> At the early stages, it is very important to get the fundamentals in both the biological fields and the computer science fields. There is no getting away from that. A lot of what people need is available right now in the traditional curricula; you can piece

together classes in molecular biology, genetics, statistics, programming, database classes, and algorithm classes. Personally, I think that it is the people who have the background in both of those areas that are going be able to make the biggest contributions. It is sometimes a stretch for students to get depth in both areas, but I think this is important for students to do.

Another thing is networking. Find out where bioinformatics is done in the community and, if you find the time, go to the talks . . . and other forums. Don't be shy to go up after someone has spoken, introduce yourself and let them know you are interested. Or, check the web pages of your professors to see what their research is about, and talk to them outside of class. Networking is really important. There are many opportunities for students to dive in and learn from the inside what is going on if they make the right contacts. This can be a better use of a student's time than loading up on extra courses. It is important to get the perspective from the inside.

On the Job

Employers

Bioinformatics specialists work in companies that develop new drugs and disease treatments and in companies that do genome sequencing and genetic research. A few of the companies that hire bioinformatics specialists include chemical and pharmaceutical companies and those doing genetic research. One job listing on Indeed.com for Qiagen, a mining company, notes the job requirements for a bioinformatics scientist: "The Bioinformatics Scientist will analyze gene expression measurements . . . and DNA sequencing reads to support new product development. This position requires adapting existing algorithms and developing new algorithms for optimal use with specific data types and specific scientific problems. The position requires a strong combination of statistical analysis skill, biology knowledge, and programming ability."

Working Conditions

Depending on whether they teach in a university and do research or work on research in a lab, bioinformatics specialists spend most of their time indoors in a lab or academic setting. Brinkman describes some of his tasks in the lab. He works with other scientists "to improve our programs that do things like automatically find mutations, or store patient data. I also try and make it a point every day to review some the bioinformatics newsgroups and journals to keep up on things that will make my job easier. Finally it seems I'm always writing tiny scripts of one sort or another to do one-off kinds of things like move a whole bunch of sequence data around that we just got from a collaborator, or blast another huge chunk of sequence looking for similarity to one gene of interest."

Earnings

Depending on the position and the degree, bioinformatics specialists can make as little as $25,000 a year or more than $100,000 a year, according to Vault.com, a career website. Bioinformatics specialists with higher degrees, such as a master's or PhD, earn more.

Opportunities for Advancement

Many bioinformatics specialists begin their careers as bioinformatics technicians whose job is to help a more experienced researcher. From there, they may advance to an entry level bioinformatics specialist position. After three to five years, they might move on to become experienced bioinformatics specialists working on more difficult projects with more responsibility, and then become either supervisors, managers, or college professors.

What Is the Future Outlook for Bioinformatics Specialists?

The relative newness of the field along with the specialized skills required means a lot of opportunity for bioinformatics specialists. Vault.com predicts a 3 to 9 percent growth rate through 2020. The most opportunity will be available for those with a higher-level education. Eleazar Eskin, professor of bioinformatics at the University of California, Los Angeles, agrees. He was interviewed on the website guidetoonlineschools.com.

There are huge opportunities for graduate programs in Bioinformatics because of the current growth of these programs and the relatively small number of applicants. Beyond graduate school, there is now a large biotech industry that is interested in hiring individuals with experience in bioinformatics. Since a lot of the training in bioinformatics is in computational problem solving, bioinformatics graduates are well prepared for careers outside of bioinformatics as well. Our graduates are in a great position to work in any area of data analysis. These days with "big data" being a hot topic, there are plenty of jobs available for the graduates.

Find Out More

The Bioinformatics Organization, Inc.
website: bioinformatics.org

The Bioinformatics Organization, Inc. is an online resource that serves the scientific and educational needs of bioinformatic practitioners and the general public. It develops and maintains computational resources to facilitate world-wide communications and collaborations between people of all educational and professional levels.

International Association of Engineers (IAENG)
Unit 1, 1/F, 37-39 Hung To Rd.
Hong Kong
China
website: IAENG.org

The IAENG is a nonprofit international association for engineers and computer scientists. It promotes cooperation between professionals in various fields of engineering and the advancement and development of technology. The IAENG Society of Bioinformatics specifically serves engineers and scholars in the bioinformatics discipline.

International Society for Clinical Biostatistics (ISCB)
ISCB Permanent Office
Bregnerodvej 132 A
DK-3460 Birkerod, Denmark
phone: +45 26 82 79 70
website: ISCB.info

The International Society for Clinical Biostatistics was founded in 1978 to stimulate research into the principles and methodology used in the design and analysis of clinical research and to increase the relevance of statistical theory to the real world of clinical medicine.

International Society for Computational Biology
9500 Gilman Dr., MC 0505
UCSD/SDSC
La Jolla, CA 92093-0505
phone: (858) 822-0852
website: ISCB.org

The International Society for Computational Biology addresses scientific policies, providing access to high quality publications, organizing meetings, and serving as a portal to information about training, education, employment, and news from related fields.

Medical and Clinical Laboratory Technologist

What Does a Medical and Clinical Laboratory Technologist Do?

At a Glance:

Medical and Clinical Laboratory Technologist

Minimum Educational Requirements
Bachelor's degree in medical technology or life sciences

Personal Qualities
Technology-minded; dexterous; detail oriented; physical and mental stamina

Certification and Licensing
May be required by some states

Working Conditions
Indoors in lab setting; may stand for long periods

Salary Range
Approximately $24,790, to $57,710

Number of Jobs
As of 2012 about 325,800

Future Job Outlook
Growth of 14 percent through 2022

Medical technologists are a key part of any medical laboratory and surgical center. Every test that is ordered by a physician passes through the hands of or is supervised by a medical technologist. They are the link between the doctor who is attempting to diagnose a problem and the diagnosis. They perform tests using complex machines that perform chemical, biological, hematological, immunological, microscopic, and bacteriological analyses. They rarely have contact with patients, yet their work is critical to helping patients get well. One unnamed medical technologist interviewed on citytowninfo.com works in a hospital in southern New Hampshire. She describes the importance of the work: "A medical technologist is a vital part of a hospital's staff. I am the person behind the scenes. Every lab test that a doctor orders comes to the laboratory where a medical technologist puts it through a series of screenings. The results are often the key to a patient's diagnosis and contain invaluable information."

Medical technologists perform many surprising duties, including using a microscope to examine blood and other bodily fluids. They can also cross-match blood for transfusions and determine levels of glucose and cholesterol.

They may also take tissue samples to determine the presence of bacteria, fungi, parasites, or antibodies. They do this by mixing these samples with particular nutrients that allow the samples to grow, to more readily determine what is infecting a patient. The medical technologist quoted in citytowninfo.com explains the importance of these tests from a practical point of view:

> Many types of patient samples come into the lab. Blood samples can be tested for numerous things. In hematology, blood is tested both manually and with machines. Red blood cell counts, white blood cell counts, hemoglobin and hematocrit levels are determined here. Slides are made with the patient's blood so techs can look at the cells under a microscope to see if they look normal or abnormal. Abnormal cells are often an indication of specific diseases like mono or different types of leukemia or cancer.

> Another part of the lab is called urinalysis and coagulation. Here we test urine for abnormalities and blood for coagulation problems. In microbiology samples are tested for bacteria. Throat swabs can be tested for strep throat. Urine is tested for bacteria which can aid in the detection of a urinary tract infection. Blood is tested for bacteria as well, a test that is crucial to determining if a very sick person is septic.

> The blood bank is a very exciting part of the lab. Here we test patients' blood types and get blood ready for transfusion. . . . A blood banker can save a patient's life by getting blood ready quick enough to be infused.

Medical technologists do more than just perform tests, however. They evaluate the tests for the doctor and give the doctor the results. They also are in charge of laboratory procedure to guarantee that everyone performs tests in a similar manner to ensure the accuracy of the results.

Carrie Leyh is a medical technologist at LabCorp Dynacare in Seattle, Washington. She specializes in microbiology and is interviewed in onlinebiologydegree.com. She says that her typical day starts with readying the equipment that will be used during the day: "At the beginning of the day, I perform tasks such as performing maintenance on the machines and diagnostic equipment as well as making sure the machines are set at the correct temperature with the correct atmosphere requirements for the organisms. Then I transition into determining the diagnosis of inpatient and outpatient samples by doing cultures and running a variety of tests. I also run sensitivities to determine what antibiotics, antivirals or antifungals are needed to cure the patient."

For people who enjoy participating in the medical field but may not have the aptitude, desire, or financial means to spend years obtaining a medical degree, the job of medical technologist could be a good choice.

How Do You Become a Medical and Clinical Laboratory Technologist?

Education

Medical technologists need a bachelor's degree, but while obtaining a BA in medical technology is possible at some schools, a student can also obtain a degree in one of the sciences such as chemistry or biology. Students choosing a medical technology degree take courses in chemistry, biological sciences, microbiology, mathematics, and statistics, as well as courses designed to teach knowledge and skills used in the clinical laboratory. Leyh explains that a student wanting to take on this career should make an important early decision: "I would tell a student interested in becoming a medical technologist to figure out

A laboratory technologist reviews test results. Technologists perform tests and evaluate them, providing an important link between the doctor who is attempting to diagnose a problem and the diagnosis.

whether they want to be a generalist or specialist in the medical field. Some students choose to specialize in chemistry because they have an interest in blood work, while other students opt to specialize in pathology because they want to work with tissues. However, I would encourage students to consider becoming a generalist. Being a general medical technologist allows you to explore different departments and perform a wide array of tests in the laboratory."

If a student does not major in science, he or she can still pursue the career by opting for post-baccalaureate training. Some of these educational programs take twelve months to complete; others take eighteen months. The credential earned is usually known as a Medical Laboratory Technology Certificate of Proficiency, though it has other names. Classes cover medical microbiology, clinical chemistry, phlebotomy, hematology, parasitology, diagnostic immunology, and clinical laboratory instrumentation. These programs are often accredited by a national organization such as the Commission on Accreditation of Allied Health Education Programs (CAAHEP) or the National Accrediting Agency for Clinical Laboratory Sciences.

Certification and Licensing

Though optional, some states require certification of lab workers. Several organizations offer certification programs, including the American Medical Technologists. In order to maintain licenses and certifications, medical technologists must complete continuing education requirements. The type and amount varies according to the credentialing. The American Medical Technologist certification status mandates forty-five continuing education credits within a three-year period. Most states require up to fifteen continuing education units each year to maintain a license in medical technology.

Volunteer Work and Internships

Medical technologists agree that practical lab experience before graduation is key to finding a position. Many colleges, especially those either with medical technology degree programs or those that offer the Medical Laboratory Technology Certificate of Proficiency program, offer internships in a laboratory setting.

Skills and Personality

Because their work involves accurate testing and analysis, medical technologists must be extremely organized and detail oriented. They also must enjoy problem solving. They work long hours, sometimes on their feet, in an indoor lab setting, so they must be able to tolerate working in an enclosed area. However, their job has a lot of variety and a feeling of being a vital part of the workings of a hospital or lab. Medical technologists must also enjoy science and math. Judy Gust, a medical technologist in the laboratory at St. Joseph's Hospital in St. Paul, Minnesota, describes the requirements in an interview in the *Minneapolis StarTribune* website, startribune.com:

> In college, I loved biology and chemistry. My advisor was a former med tech who told me it would be ever-changing. I've always been glad that she steered me in this direction. Med techs have a lot of options besides the hospital. They can work

in clinics, industries, blood centers, public health, research, pharmaceutical companies and crime labs. If you watch CSI, that's what we do. . . . It's challenging and involves a lot of problem-solving. Every day there is something different. I really feel like my daily job has an immediate impact on the care of the patient. There are a lot of opportunities to grow and develop within the career. It's never the same. There's always something new. Things develop so fast that it's really exciting. You have to love change.

On the Job

Employers

The Bureau of Labor Statistics lists the industries that employed the most medical laboratory technologists and technicians. General medical and surgical hospitals at the state, local, and private level employed 50 percent of medical laboratory technologists and technicians. Medical and diagnostic laboratories employed 17 percent, physician offices employed 10 percent, while colleges and universities employed 5 percent.

Working Conditions

Most medical technologists work full time, though part-time positions are available. Because some labs are open twenty-four hours a day, technologists can work different shifts, including second shift. Though the work is not physically strenuous, it is painstaking and requires attention to detail. An unnamed medical technologist from Chicago, Illinois, writes about the conditions on the Indeed.com website job forum: "The most challenging part about the profession is working the long hours, which are required to take a job that pays the bills, and turn it into a job to obtain the things you want. Overtime potential, and working a second job are great ways to supplement your income, but they cut into your social life. . . . I'm a 3 year tech, and learning the path to be a successful scientist is challenging to say the least, but once you learn the path, and if you keep up to date on the policy and procedure changes—you can be an extremely effective tech, and after a while it seems you kick on the autopilot, and work becomes simple."

Earnings

According to the Bureau of Labor Statistics, the median annual wage for medical laboratory technologists was $57,580 in May 2012. The lowest 10 percent earned less than $39,580, and the highest 10 percent earned more than $78,900.

Opportunities for Advancement

Advancement opportunities for medical technologists generally follow from years on the job and specific aptitudes that each individual may develop. Medical technologists can be supervisors, move into more complex research jobs that involve developing new tests, and they may enjoy teaching less experienced medical technologists. One example of a career track is provided by the world-renowned Mayo Clinic, with locations in Minnesota, Arizona, and Florida. It offers medical technologists several different advancement tracks, including development technologist, technical, education, and management, all depending on the interests of the technologist. For example, Joel chose the technical track and became an equipment specialist in the special coagulation laboratory: "I began work at Mayo Clinic in 1997 as a Medical Technologist in the Special Coagulation Laboratory. I am currently the equipment specialist and am responsible for maintaining and resolving problems for all of the lab's equipment. I troubleshoot the equipment myself, work with the lab services group, or communicate with the instrument manufacturer. I also work at the bench approximately two or three days a week when needed." Larger hospital facilities have larger labs and more opportunities.

What Is the Future Outlook for Medical and Clinical Laboratory Technologists?

According to the Bureau of Labor Statistics, employment of medical laboratory technologists is projected to grow 14 percent through

2022. Several factors will contribute to the growth in the profession. As more sophisticated machines are able to automate and produce testing results, medical technologists will be needed to operate the machines and be able to set up and repair them. The challenge of new infectious diseases will continue to require medical technologists to test for them. As the baby boomer population continues to age, it will be accessing health care in ever greater numbers, providing new job opportunities.

Find Out More

The American Association of Bioanalysts (AAB)
906 Olive St., Suite 1200
St. Louis, MO 63101-1448
phone: (314) 241-1445
website: aab.org

AAB is a national professional association whose members are clinical laboratory directors, owners, supervisors, managers, medical technologists, medical laboratory technicians, physician office laboratory technicians and phlebotomists. AAB is committed to the pursuit of excellence in clinical laboratory services by enhancing the professional skills of each of its members.

American Medical Technologists (AMT)
10700 W. Higgins Rd., Suite 150
Rosemont, IL 60018
phone: (800) 275-1268
website: americanmedtech.org

The mission of AMT is to manage, promote, expand upon, and continuously improve certification programs for allied health professionals who work in a variety of disciplines and settings, to administer certification examinations, and to provide continuing education, information, advocacy services, and other benefits to members.

The American Society for Clinical Laboratory Science (ASCLS)
1861 International Dr., Suite 200
McLean, VA 22102
phone: (571) 748-3770
website: ascls.org

The mission of ASCLS is to make a positive impact in health care through leadership that will assure excellence in the practice of laboratory medicine. ASCLS works to define the characteristics of competent personnel within the profession and provide professional development opportunities.

The American Society for Clinical Pathology (ASCP)
33 W. Monroe St., Suite 1600
Chicago, IL 60603
phone: (312) 541-4999
website: ascp.org

ASCP is the world's largest professional membership organization for pathologists and laboratory professionals. ASCP's mission is to provide excellence in education, certification, and advocacy on behalf of patients, pathologists, and laboratory professionals across the globe.

Interview with a Biological Technician

Miranda Brett is a part-time biological technician with the California Department of Fish and Wildlife (CDFW) Fisheries Branch. She has held this job since January 2013. The author interviewed her via e-mail.

Q: Why did you become a biological technician?

A: I became a biological technician because it is a fun job that allows me to gain research and fieldwork experience as I strive toward a career in biological or fisheries research. In the past I have worked as a research technician for SDSU [San Diego State University], working on a variety of research projects for a professor. I'm currently working as a technician for the CDFW Fisheries Branch. After graduating with a B.S. in Biology, it is a very competitive workforce and technician positions are the perfect introductory jobs in the field that allow you to gain valuable experiences and skill sets on a variety of projects.

Q: Can you describe your typical workday?

A: There isn't really a typical workday, which is what makes the job so exciting. It really varies depending [on] what kind of projects are going on. For example, right now we are doing a population estimate at Lake Castaic. So every Saturday we monitor the bass tournaments and clip all of the caught bass and mark all caught and recaptured bass. Other typical days include putting dead trees into lakes to create structural habitat for the fish, performing angler surveys to monitor fishermen's catches, working in the lab fish scales, hiking and backpack electrofishing mountain streams to identify fish species. A typical day while working as a technician for the university varied between working in the lab sorting and identifying small invertebrates under a microscope and working in the field scuba diving to collect data and conduct experiments.

Q: What do you like most and least about your job?

A: The most fun about the job is the amount of time I get to spend in the field. As a technician you are on the bottom of the rank but get to experience a wide range of projects and collect the data. My favorite fieldwork for this specific position is electrofishing. This is where we go out on lakes on electrofishing boats to collect fish typically for a general fish survey. The boat has anodes and cathodes attached that send an electrical current in the water that stuns the fish. This allows us to net the fish, and bring them into the boat to collect measurements, scales or whatever information we need and then release the fish back into the water unharmed.

The least fun part of the job is the data entry. Although data entry can be a monotonous, boring task it is important. It can be fun though, if you have the opportunity to take the next step past the data entry to analyze the data, make graphs and run statistics. Another data crunching task is compiling the data into report format so that it is accessible by the public. Writing reports is not a typical task of a technician but depending on who you work for can be and is a valuable skill to gain for moving up to a permanent career in the field.

Q: What personal qualities do you find most valuable for this type of work?

A: I think the biological technician category fits a range of personalities depending on the specific field the technician work is in. In general though, it is important for a technician to be hardworking, flexible and willing and excited to learn new things and tasks. I also believe it is important for a technician to be striving for a career in the field. This allows you to gain the most from the job. Typically, technician positions are perfect for recent graduates or students that want real fieldwork experience.

Q: What advice do you have for students who might be interested in this career?

A: This is the perfect job to try out and see what kind of lab or fieldwork you are interested in, in the field of biology. If you are applying for a technician position and at first do not get the job because you don't have enough experience in the field, I recommend asking to volunteer. Typically, technician positions are working for environmental scientists or biologists who started out working as technicians and understand that position. They can usually use extra helping hands during field expeditions so volunteering will demonstrate to them you're hardworking and able to perform the job. That is what got me the job.

Other Jobs in Biotechnology

Agricultural and Food Scientists
Animal Caretaker
Animal Technician
Biological Forensic Analyst
Biologist
Bioprocess Engineer
Biosafety Regulator
Biostatistician
Clinical Pharmacist
Clinical Research Associate
Conservation Geneticist
Documentation Coordinator
Drug Safety Specialist
Environmental Biotechnologist
Enzymologist
Fermentation Scientist
Forensic DNA Analyst
Greenhouse and Field
  Technician
Greenhouse and Field Worker

Health and Safety Specialist
Human Geneticist
Immunologist
Instrumentation/Calibration
  Technician
Laboratory Assistant
Laboratory Automation
  Specialist
Laboratory Support Worker
Manufacturing Assistant
Manufacturing Technician
Material Handler
Medical Biochemist
Process Engineer
Quality Assurance Specialist
Quality Control Technician
Regulatory Affairs Specialist
Research Associate
Sales Representative
Zoologist

Editor's Note: The online *Occupational Outlook Handbook* of the US Department of Labor's Bureau of Labor Statistics is an excellent source of information on jobs in hundreds of career fields including many of those listed here. The *Occupational Outlook Handbook* may be accessed online at www.bls.gov/ooh/.

Index